Summary of

Monopoly in Money and Inflation
The Case for a Constitution to Discipli~

H. GEOFFREY BRENNAN a~

1. The argument of 'market failu~
   only a governmental rôle in~
   support a government monopo~

2. The process has been aided by ~ ⌐ut naïve assumption that governments are 'be..⌐ent despots'; in reality politicians are not above self-seeking and have tended throughout the ages to abuse their money-creation authority.

3. Standard monopoly theory can be extended to governments to show that they will maximise the real revenues they can extract from an unrestricted monopoly power to issue money.

4. Money is valued as an instrument for facilitating future exchanges. Thus the real value to governments of the money issue will be the *transactions* value, which can be secured in full by them in a non-inflationary régime.

5. But governments can extract more than the pure transactions value of money by reducing the capital value of individuals' cash balances through inflationary new currency issues.

6. There are clearly feedback constraints on governments' propensity to inflate away the capital value of money balances— the limiting case being the return to a wholly barter economy as a rational response to full anticipation of the *confiscation* of capital values.

7. Economic theory shows there will always be some rate of inflation which will secure for governments more real revenue than in a simple non-inflationary régime.

8. Recognition that governments are self-seeking monopolistic revenue-maximisers leads to the conclusion that they must be constrained by *rules* under a monetary constitution.

9. Unrestrained monetary monopoly is the *institutional* explanation of the great inflation of the 1970s, and demands *institutional* reform. It is the monetary *régime*, not monetary *policy*, which must be changed.

10. Several schemes have been proposed whose rules amount to a form of monetary constitution. But as a first step, agreement on the need for a constitution is more important than its precise content.

Hobart Paper 88 is published (price £1.50) by

THE INSTITUTE OF ECONOMIC AFFAIRS
2 Lord North Street, Westminster
London SW1P 3LB   Telephone: 01-799 3745

IEA PUBLICATIONS

Subscription Service

An annual subscription is the most convenient way to obtain our publications. Every title we produce in all our regular series will be sent to you immediately on publication and without further charge, representing a substantial saving.

*Subscription rates**

Britain: £15.00 p.a. including postage.

£14.00 p.a. if paid by Banker's Order.

£10.00 p.a. teachers and students who pay *personally*.

Europe and South America: 40 US dollars or equivalent.

Other countries: Rates on application. In most countries subscriptions are handled by local agents.

*These rates are *not* available to companies or to institutions.

To: The Treasurer, Institute of Economic Affairs,
2 Lord North Street,
Westminster, London SW1P 3LB.

I should like to subscribe beginning.....................................
I enclose a cheque/postal order for:

☐ £15.00

☐ Please send me a Banker's Order form

☐ Please send me an Invoice

☐ £10.00 [I am a teacher/student at................................]

Name..

Address...

....

Signed..   Date.................

Monopoly in Money and Inflation

*The Case for a Constitution
to Discipline Government*

H. GEOFFREY BRENNAN

and

JAMES M. BUCHANAN

Published by

THE INSTITUTE OF ECONOMIC AFFAIRS

1981

First published in January 1981

ⓒ THE INSTITUTE OF ECONOMIC AFFAIRS 1981

ISSN 0073-2818
ISBN 0-255 36138-6

Printed in England by

GORON PRO-PRINT CO LTD

6 Marlborough Road, Churchill Industrial Estate, Lancing, Sussex

Text set in 'Monotype' Baskerville

CONTENTS

page

PREFACE   *Arthur Seldon*   7

THE AUTHORS   11

PART I:

Setting the Stage: The Politics of Money   13

1. THE LITTLE ALCHEMIST: TWO VERSIONS
   OF A FABLE   15
   Version A   15
   Version B   15
   Alchemist not foolish: government foolish?   16

2. BUT 'MONEY IS DIFFERENT'   16
   Free competition in money may not
   guarantee efficiency   17
   Governmental monetary function thought
   necessary because of inherent market
   'instability'   18

3. AND 'GOVERNMENT IS BENEVOLENT'   19
   Keynesian fiscal policy creates bias towards
   deficits   19
   Pervasiveness of the 'benevolent despot'
   image   20

4. DEMOCRATIC ELECTORAL CONSTRAINTS ON
   GOVERNMENT   21
   'Public choice' analysis shows weakness of
   democratic restraints on government   22

5. GOVERNMENT AS MONOPOLIST   22
   Economic theory of monopoly applied to
   governmental monetary behaviour   24

[3]

PART II:

Analysis: Unrestrained Government Monopoly in Creating Money   27

6. MONOPOLY FRANCHISES IN MONEY CREATION   29
International influences on domestic money monopolist   29

7. TRANSACTIONS VALUE OF MONEY IN A NON-INFLATIONARY ECONOMY   30
Real capital value of monopolistic money issue   31
Possible behaviour of a 'do-gooding' government money monopolist   32

8. REAL REVENUE POTENTIAL IN EXCESS OF TRANSACTIONS VALUE   32
Full transactions value of money   33
The limits to the monetary monopolist's real revenue   34

9. BUT THE PEOPLE CANNOT BE FOOLED ALL THE TIME   35
Analytical usefulness of assumption of individual rationality   35

10. THE CREDIBILITY DILEMMA   36
Unexploited 'gains-from-trade'   37

11. THE DISCOUNT RATE FOR GOVERNMENT   38
Portfolio adjustment   38
The permanence of the franchise   39
Incentive to inflation of 'temporary' democratic government   40

12. REVENUE-MAXIMISING INFLATION WHEN COMMITMENTS ARE HONOURED AND WHEN INDIVIDUALS EXPECT THEM TO BE HONOURED   41
The costs to individuals of holding cash   42

13. THE GREAT MONETARY GAME   44
The monetary game is 'unfair'   44
Tax on beer contrasted with 'tax' on money   45
People learn to offset the actions of the inflationary monetary monopolist: towards a contractual approach?   46

[4]

14. MONETARY MONOPOLY AND DEPOSIT BANKING   47
     Can monopoly of money work with a competitive deposit banking system?   47
     Reserve ratio control gives power to impose capital levies on banks   48

15. MONEY CREATIONS, PUBLIC DEBT AND INCOME TAXES   48
     All debtors, including government, benefit from unexpected inflation   49
     Inflation raises real government revenue from progressive income tax   49

PART III:

The Implications for Policy   51

16. THE 'ILLEGITIMACY' OF UNCONSTRAINED MONETARY MONOPOLY   53
     Criteria for evaluating basic social/economic institutions   53
     Voluntary agreement for unconstrained monetary monopoly would be impossible   54

17. LEGALLY-PROTECTED AND UNCONSTRAINED MONOPOLY IN PRODUCTION OR SALE   55
     Unregulated legal monopoly causes net social welfare loss   55
     Natural monopoly and legal enforcement   56

18. WHY HAS MONEY BEEN TREATED DIFFERENTLY?   57
     Economists have been uncritical of government monopoly in money   57

19. MONETARY ARRANGEMENTS TO MEET CONSTITUTIONAL TESTS   58
     (i) Free market in money, with no governmental rôle   59
         Behaviour of government money monopolist crucial to choice between it and free markets in money   59

(ii)   Governmental money issue, but competi-
       tive entry   60
(iii) Pure commodity money, with govern-
       mental definition of value   61
(iv)   Fiat money issue constrained by consti-
       tutional rules   62
       Monetary indexing for stability   62

20. THE THREE STAGES OF MONETARY DEBATES   63
(i)   Discretionary monetary policy   63
(ii)   The desirable monetary constitution   64
(iii) The desirability of a monetary constitution   64
       Constitutional restraints, not 'advice',
       the only effective discipline on
       politicians   65

QUESTIONS FOR DISCUSSION   66

FURTHER READING   67

PREFACE

The *Hobart Papers* are intended to contribute a stream of authoritative, independent and lucid analyses to the understanding and application of economics to private and government activity. The characteristic theme has been the optimum use of scarce resources and the extent to which it can best be achieved in markets within an appropriate framework or, where markets cannot work, in other ways. Since in the real world the alternative to the market is the state, and both are imperfect, the choice between them should effectively depend on judgement of the comparative consequences of 'market failure' and 'government failure'.

A new form of government failure that economists are examining with increasing intensity is in the supply of money. For 200 years or more economists have generally supposed that one of the main functions of government was to provide the medium of exchange in which transactions in the market could be conducted. (Money also had other functions.) And even when the failure of government in various countries to maintain the value of money in the periods of inflation of the 19th and 20th centuries were closely debated by economists, the task was assumed to be that of helping government to control the supply of money so that it would not debase its value. Economists thus attempted to devise methods of linking the value of money to a commodity such as gold that was as far as possible beyond the influence of government.

The focus of interest is now increasingly whether government will ever be able to provide a dependable means of exchange, and whether some other method of organising the supply of money may have to be evolved. In 1976 the Institute published a pioneering *Paper* by Professor F. A. Hayek in which he argued that the only way to ensure that the value of money was maintained would be to take it out of the control of government as the sole source and put it into the market where competing suppliers would be induced to maintain the value of their individual currency by limiting its supply. The *Paper* was entitled *Denationalisation of Money* because it is government that

[7]

has 'nationalised' money and so created a monopoly in its supply. Professor Hayek's argument was essentially against the *monopoly* control of money as such, whether by government or in a private banking system, and that it was *competition* in the supply of money that would prevent its debasement.

In Hobart Paper 88 Professors Geoffrey Brennan and James M. Buchanan take the argument further by refining the conditions in which government can best be deprived of the power to control money by monopoly. Like other papers from the fertile centre of learning in Blacksburg, Virginia, where they teach, and like the other works of Professor Buchanan, Hobart Paper 88 extends the analysis beyond the stage it has reached so far, not least by applying what in the USA is called 'public choice' analysis and in Britain 'the economics of politics',[1] of which Professor Buchanan is a founding father. Most of the text should be understood by non-economists, who can skip the more technical discussion in Part II, especially Sections 7 and 8.

The *Hobart Paper* begins by doubting the realism of supposing that government can be left to control the supply of money without regard for its political interests. It rejects the notion that government will invariably use its power, in controlling money or anything else, to serve only the public interest. It argues that, consciously or unconsciously, we have supposed that government comprises benevolent despots whose motives and objectives did not have to be questioned since there was no conflict between the interests of the despots and the interests of the people.

This unrealistic, naïve, or romantic notion about the rôle of government, which made little allowance for the everyday political pressures in the working of party politics, reached its apogee in the teaching of Keynes, or, more correctly, in the teaching of the economists who claimed to interpret his teaching when he was no longer able to rebut their claims. The implied assumption of the Keynesians was that government could be left to provide the required medium of exchange by varying its supply in booms and slumps, creating or destroying it so as to maintain stability of demand, employment and income. The unreality of the supposition that government would or could be neutral in its control of money was demonstrated in Hobart Paper 78, *The Consequences of Mr Keynes*, in which Professor

---

[1] J. M. Buchanan *et al.*, *The Economics of Politics*, IEA Readings No. 18, IEA, 1978.

Buchanan collaborated with an American colleague at Blacksburg, Professor R. E. Wagner, and with a British economist now at the University of Birmingham, John Burton.

The present *Hobart Paper* discusses the reasons why the supposition is unrealistic and ends by considering methods of removing or minimising the power of government in the control of money. Professors Brennan and Buchanan discuss four main possible reforms: the issue by government of a fiat ('faith' or paper) money disciplined by a constitutional rule, a money issued by government but linked to a commodity to define its value, a money issued by government but disciplined by competition from privately-issued monies, and a free market in money with no government rôle at all. The authors favour constitutional discipline. Whatever method finally emerges from the discussion in the years ahead, the importance of the analysis is that it develops the process of considering how far government must be removed from supplying money, and how far it is possible by constitutional disciplines to prevent government from disrupting the supply of money and thereby the working of the economy as a whole.

In the course of the discussion the authors touch on a conundrum now causing much anxiety in Britain: how to ensure that the authorities know and use the techniques that will effectively control the supply of money to master inflation. They say that a fiat money issued by government could be disciplined by constitutional rules defined either in terms of the *supply* of money or of the *value* of the unit of money. The former kind of rule has been proposed by Professor Friedman, who has argued that the supply of money should be related to the rate of economic growth. The second, proposed by economists of an earlier day, Irving Fisher and Henry Simons, argued that the monetary authority should keep the value of the monetary unit stable in terms of an index of prices. The advantage of the Friedman-type rule is that it is applied well before the increase in prices is due, although it may not be able to allow for unforeseen other influences on the course of prices. The advantage of the Fisher-Simons-type rule is that it can allow for unpredicted emergence of substitutes for money, such as credit cards, but it is more difficult to monitor since the adjustment takes place after the rise in prices and may be too late.

It may be that in the 1980s, when there are more substitutes for money and, not least, when money is increasingly not used at all because barter is used to evade taxation, there will have to be more refined experimentation in the constitutional rules required to ensure that the monetary authority avoids or masters inflation.

The Institute's constitution requires it to preclude its Trustees, Advisers and Directors from necessarily accepting the analysis or conclusions of its published work, but it presents Professors Brennan and Buchanan's *Hobart Paper* as an original contribution to the developing re-appraisal of the function of government in the supply of money and therefore in the economy of a free society.

December 1980   ARTHUR SELDON

THE AUTHORS

H. GEOFFREY BRENNAN was born in 1944 and educated at Broken Hill High School and the Australian National University, Canberra (BEc First-Class Honours 1966, PhD 1976). Professor of Economics, Virginia Polytechnic Institute and State University, since 1978. Successively Lecturer, Senior Lecturer and Reader in Public Finance, Australian National University, 1968-78. Full-time Research Consultant to the Australian Taxation Review Committee, 1973-74.

Professor Brennan's main research and teaching interests are in public finance, welfare economics and public choice. He has been a member of the editorial board of *Public Finance Quarterly* since 1975. Joint editor: *The Economics of Federalism* (A.N.U. Press, Canberra, 1980); joint author (with Professor Buchanan), *The Power to Tax: Analytical Foundations of a Fiscal Constitution* (C.U.P., 1980); author of numerous articles in the academic press (including *Journal of Political Economy*, *Public Choice*, *American Economic Review*, and *Econometrica*), and of contributions to books and conference proceedings.

He is married with three children.

JAMES McGILL BUCHANAN has been University Professor of Economics and Director of the Center for Study of Public Choice at the Virginia Polytechnic Institute, Blacksburg, Virginia, since 1969. Previously he was Professor of Economics at Florida State University, 1951-56, University of Virginia (and Director of the Thomas Jefferson Center for Political Economy), 1956-68, and University of California at Los Angeles, 1968-69.

He is the author of numerous works on aspects of the economics of politics and public choice, including *The Calculus of Consent* (with Gordon Tullock) (1962), *Public Finance in Democratic Process* (1967), *Demand and Supply of Public Goods* (1968), *Public Principles of Public Debt* (1958), *The Limits of Liberty: Between Anarchy and Leviathan* (1975), (with Richard E. Wagner) *Democracy in Deficit: The Political Legacy of Lord Keynes* (1977), *Freedom in Constitutional Contract* (1978), *What Should*

[11]

Economists Do? (1979), and (with H. Geoffrey Brennan) *The Power to Tax: Analytical Foundations of a Fiscal Constitution* (1980). Professor Buchanan is a member of the IEA's Advisory Council. The IEA has published his *The Inconsistencies of the National Health Service* (Occasional Paper 7, 1965), (with Richard E. Wagner and John Burton) *The Consequences of Mr Keynes* (Hobart Paper 78, 1978), and an essay, 'From Private Preferences to Public Philosophy: The Development of Public Choice', in *The Economics of Politics* (IEA Readings No. 18, 1978).

PART I

Setting the Stage: the Politics of Money

1. THE LITTLE ALCHEMIST: TWO VERSIONS OF A FABLE

Version A

Once upon a time, deep in the forest, there lived a little alchemist who spent all his time searching for a way to turn sand into gold. One dreary winter's day, his efforts were rewarded. He found a secret formula with which he could make all the gold he could ever want from the sand near his cottage.

The little alchemist could then make gold and exchange it for anything his heart desired. He first built a fine castle, and filled it with beautiful things. He hired many servants: maids, cooks, butlers, gardeners, and coachmen. His table was graced with gourmet foods from throughout the land. He equipped a stable with fine horses. The procession of pretty ladies who came to visit the castle suggested to some rather cynical observers that the little alchemist used his gold to purchase almost anything.

All the other people in the land were made poorer by the alchemist's discovery, since they gave up the goods and the labour that went into building the castle, training the fine horses, growing and eating the food, and even the pleasure of the fine ladies. Those others did not, of course, realise that the new gold made by the little alchemist simply reduced the exchange value of all the other gold in the land, which had been, for ages, used for money.

Version B

The little alchemist discovered the secret formula for turning sand into gold. But, before he made any gold, he decided to put on his economics thinking cap. He wanted to consider the effects of his discovery on all the people in the land. The little alchemist understood that he could, if desired, make gold and use it to buy all the good things he wanted. But he also understood that these things would have to come from somebody; others would have to give up the goods and labour to satisfy

[15]

his desires. While he would become very rich, others in the land would become poorer. Since the little alchemist *cared about other people* as well as himself, he decided not to use his discovery at all. He did not make even so much as one ounce of gold from sand. He built no fine castle; he hired no servants. Instead, he destroyed the secret formula, never again to be found.

Alchemist not foolish: government foolish?

What would a girl of 10 say if we read our two versions of the fable to her? She would accept the first, but probably reject the second as totally 'untrue'. No little alchemist would be so foolish as to destroy his means of getting very rich.

Nonetheless, sophisticated thinkers are not supposed to have the wisdom of the 10-year-old, because the second version is precisely the sort of story we have all been supposed to believe for centuries whenever questions about the authority of governments to print money are raised. If we do nothing more than replace the words 'little alchemist' by 'government', and the word 'gold' by 'paper money' in the fable, the similarity becomes self-evident. Government possesses the power to create money and exchange it for goods and services, but we are supposed to believe it will use this power only in the 'public interest', and refrain from using it to purchase the things it may desire.

The fable of the little alchemist helps us to get a realistic perspective on government and inflation. If government has the power to create something without cost that will enable it to purchase things it wants, surely childlike wisdom would suggest that such power will be used. Why has this self-evident proposition been so widely overlooked and misunderstood throughout the ages? Why have very intelligent men and women been led to accept the unrealistic version of the fable?

2. BUT 'MONEY IS DIFFERENT'

There are two parts of the answer to this question. The first would suggest that 'money is different' (below), the second that 'government is benevolent' (Section 3, pp. 19-21).

Economists have emphasised that money is indeed different from ordinary goods and services. We do not have to master the intricacies of monetary theory to appreciate that money serves a quite different function from that of an ordinary commodity. We do not 'eat money' or 'wear it on our back'. Money is useful because it facilitates the operation of the whole economy. It has often been referred to as the 'grease' that makes the economic wheels go around.

Free competition in money may not guarantee efficiency

This difference in function does not, however, necessarily suggest that the competitive market economy, within a framework of law, would not or could not operate so that something would emerge as 'money' which would be supplied and demanded like other commodities and services. Even in the total absence of governmental action, money would emerge in some form. But economists have argued, with considerable persuasiveness, that money is different also in the sense that free competition may not guarantee efficiency.

Suppose there were a régime of 'free entry into money creation'. Anyone could set up a bank and begin to accept deposits, make loans, and issue bank notes. Such a régime might be highly vulnerable to waves of expansion and contraction.

The conjectural history of the goldsmith illustrates the argument. The goldsmith takes his clients' gold pieces for safe-keeping. Experience teaches him that only a small proportion of his clients will demand a return of their deposits on any particular day. Therefore, he commences to lend out a portion of these deposits, holding only a fraction of gold in reserve, designed to meet demands for return by depositors. In so doing, the goldsmith 'creates' new money. Both the old and the new depositors treat the same gold as money for their purposes. But there may come a day when a disproportionately large number of depositors simultaneously demand a return of their initial deposits of gold pieces. The goldsmith cannot honour all claims. Evidence of this incapacity will, in turn, cause still other depositors to present their claims. There will be a 'run' on the bank which, spread throughout the economy, would mean financial crisis.

There seems to be nothing in the competitive-market structure to keep the supply of money in the economy from being expanded too rapidly in 'fair weather' and contracted too

[17]

sharply in 'foul weather'. Because of the peculiarities of money, the competitive market will 'fail'. A governmental rôle in defining and/or regulating the value of the monetary unit seems to follow from the demonstration.

The minimally-required governmental rôle may be limited to designating a specific commodity, gold or silver, or some other commodity (or combination of commodities) as the money unit, along with a pledge to purchase and sell it for a fixed price. The forces of the competitive economy would, in this setting, continue to be relied on to generate supplies of the monetary commodity in line with demands at the fixed price or value. This essentially was the idealised model considered relevant during the 19th-century heyday of the international gold standard. Even then the system did not work as well as the simple model might have predicted, largely because of the fractional reserve basis for monetary expansion and contraction that remained (the amount of paper money permitted was a percentage of the gold reserves).

Governmental monetary function thought necessary because of inherent market 'instability'

In this century, a somewhat different argument has been used to support a much more active rôle for government in monetary matters. The competitive market economy may be inherently unstable, it is argued, even if we disregard the monetary sources of instability. In this basically Keynesian or post-Keynesian approach, a governmental responsibility for promoting stability in income and in employment seems to follow. And many governments were assigned this rôle after the Great Depression of the 1930s.

To meet this responsibility, it is said, government must have tools to influence aggregate demand or aggregate spending. Hence, government should be granted authority to issue and to destroy money. This money-issue power offers an effective means of increasing aggregate demand during periods of depression, either by direct government spending or by the distribution of cash, and of reducing aggregate demand during periods of inflation. A government without such powers might be severely handicapped in trying to fulfil its stabilisation rôle. (Note that this argument is used to justify much more than a governmental rôle in setting a *fixed* value on some designated monetary commodity.)

[18]

3. AND 'GOVERNMENT IS BENEVOLENT'

The 'market failure' argument, in either one of the two forms noted, has been used to justify governmental intervention in the regulation of the economy's monetary affairs. The demonstration of market failure does not itself, however, justify a governmental rôle. To do so, it must be accompanied by analysis and demonstration of how government will act in carrying out the rôle assigned to it. In the absence of some view of how the political-governmental process works, 'market failure' provides no grounds for the delegation of money creation authority to government. This elementary methodological truth has been overlooked and/or neglected by far too many modern economists, political scientists, sociologists, and other social scientists. Almost without consideration, economists who have discussed questions of economic policy, including monetary institutions, have accepted implicitly what can only be called an unrealistic, naïve, unhistorical, Utopian, 'benevolent despot' image of government.

This 'benevolent despot' designation is convenient because economists have placed themselves in positions of proffering advice on policy reform, as if the political decision-makers, whoever these may be, will accept and act on such advice in total independence from any human motivations or impulses that political decision-makers themselves might possess. As a result of this somewhat bizarre stance, economists have made suggestions on policy proposals that totally ignore the working of politics, with the result that proposals finally adopted have often become perverted versions of the original suggestions.

Keynesian fiscal policy creates bias towards deficits

The most dramatic and the most important example is provided in the Keynesian theory of fiscal policy concerning the use of the government budget for national economic stabilisation. The Keynesian policy rule is simple: create budget deficits during periods when there is a shortfall in aggregate demand; create budget surpluses during periods when there is excessive aggregate demand. Such a policy rule, however, would only be implemented by a benevolent authoritarian political régime. In ordinary democracies, whether of the British parliamentary or the American Congressional variety, elected politicians and parties will gladly create deficits. They

[19]

like to spend; they do not enjoy levying taxes on constituents. But they will rarely, if ever, deliberately create budget surpluses. They do not like to reduce spending or to increase taxes. Even slight attention to the relevance of normal political behaviour should have suggested that the Utopian Keynesian rule for fiscal policy would produce biases towards budget deficits.[1]

As early as 1896, the great Swedish economist, Knut Wicksell, warned his colleague about the folly of assuming government to be a 'benevolent despot' in talking about matters of economic policy. He notes that such an assumption about government was likely to distract attention away from constructive reform, which must focus on prospects for changing the rules and institutions through which policy outcomes are generated from the interactions of political decision-makers who are fallible persons like the rest of us.

In the second version of our fable, the little alchemist tries to promote the general interest of the whole community. There can, in this version, be no argument for imposing restrictions on his behaviour. There may be a rôle for the economist, in this story, in pointing out the consequences of alternative actions, so that the benign little alchemist may be better informed on exactly what 'doing good' entails. More ambitiously, the social scientist *qua* moral philosopher may wish to assist the alchemist in defining what is 'good' in a more abstract sense. But there can be no argument here for restrictions on the alchemist's behaviour, for rules chosen in advance to guard against the worst possible outcomes: such restrictions can only inhibit him from carrying forward the 'public interest'.

Pervasiveness of the 'benevolent despot' image

This benevolent despot image of the political process has been pervasive in the policy attitudes of political economists. And it has naturally directed attention to the sorts of activities that make sense in the benevolent despot setting—tracing out the effects of alternative policy choices, and preaching the message of what effects are 'good'. But once we so much as admit the

---

[1] A comprehensive discussion of this bias is in James M. Buchanan and Richard E. Wagner, *Democracy in Deficit: The Political Legacy of Lord Keynes*, Academic Press, New York, 1977; for an application to Britain, James M. Buchanan, Richard Wagner, and John Burton, *The Consequences of Mr Keynes,* Hobart Paper 78, IEA, 1978.

possibility that such an image of government may be unduly optimistic, we turn naturally to consider whether there may be prospects for reform in a different direction—by changing the political institutions, the rules that govern the behaviour of political decision-makers.

Constitutional requirements for budget balance, for tax and spending limits, for restricted rules on money issue make little sense if government is assumed always to do good on its own account. It is on this basis that many accomplished, if politically naïve, economists have actively opposed such proposals. The benevolent despot image of government has simply blinded them to the need to guard against dangers that should seem real and obvious enough once they are pointed out—even to a 10-year-old!

4. DEMOCRATIC ELECTORAL CONSTRAINTS ON GOVERNMENT

Our argument that government should not be explicitly or implicitly conceived in the 'benevolent despot' image may be readily accepted. But our fable of the little alchemist may still be thought inappropriate as an analogue to governmental powers of money creation. While it may be conceded that government will not act like the little alchemist in the second version of our fable, the argument may still be made that neither will government act selfishly like our hero in the first version.

Government, it will be suggested, is not able to do as 'it' pleases. There is no 'it'. There is no monolithic entity that 'behaves' analogously to a single person. Government is a very complex interaction process in which politicians and officials participate in varying rôles. The outcomes of governmental action may not reflect the motivations of any single actor. In democratic societies, government is constrained explicitly by the voters. If those who govern on behalf of the voters should try to act contrary to the general 'public interest', or at the least as this interest might be interpreted by a majority of the voters in the electorate, they will be disciplined through the electoral process. Politicians who act contrary to voters' desires will be replaced in political office by others who will follow voters' desires more closely.

This idealised model for the operation of democratic electoral constraints on the independent powers of government has come under increasing critical scrutiny, and especially so from the research developments in 'public choice' that have emerged during the decades after World War II. Periodic elections may prove relatively ineffective in restricting the discretionary powers of agents who act for the public in decision-making rôles. Bureaucrats may be able to set the agenda for legislative actions, and the motivations of elected legislators may coincide more closely with those of the bureaucracy than with those of the voting constituency. Organised group interests may be able to use the fiscal and regulatory powers of government to promote results that explicitly run counter to the general interests of all voters.

The observed rates of growth of governments, in most Western nations since World War II, make it increasingly difficult to support any 'democratically-constrained' model of politics. Relatively few modern observers are willing to attribute the observed increases in total government fiscal and regulatory activity exclusively to the ultimate demands of voters for increased quantities of governmentally-financed goods and services. Observers have come increasingly to acknowledge that governments have some internal dynamic of their own, that they act, and grow, largely independently of the wishes of the citizenry. The 19th- and early 20th-century faith in the efficacy of electoral controls over politicians seems to have been ill-placed; and the differences, on balance, between nominally democratic régimes—as in the USA, UK, etc.—and nominally non-democratic régimes—as in the Latin American military dictatorships—seem considerably less relevant, at least for monetary and budgetary policy, than they might at one time have appeared.

5. GOVERNMENT AS MONOPOLIST

We propose to analyse government in a manner directly analogous to our first version of the fable of the self-seeking little alchemist. We shall abstract completely from democratic electoral constraints of the standard variety. Voters are taken to have no effective control over governmental policy, whether on money issue or anything else, through the ordinary electoral processes. Politicians and political parties may rotate in elected office, but such rotation does not really modify the central thrust of self-seeking governmental actions.

We need not assume that all political agents all of the time act in some narrowly-defined self-interest and contrary to their versions of the 'public interest'. Our analysis is justified even if public-spirited behaviour is widespread on the part of politicians and bureaucrats. All we need do is to allow that there may be politicians and bureaucrats who, at least on occasion, will act in accordance with what we might call their 'natural proclivities', and that these run counter to the basic desires of the citizenry. If only this much be accepted, we are warranted in trying to analyse government behaviour in the 'worst-case' setting where such natural proclivities predominate.

In a sense, our analysis is similar to that which has dominated economic-policy discussion and which was criticised above. Our supposition of 'malevolent despotism' is designed for a purpose: to offer a setting within which we can begin to discuss constructive reform in the external constraints on the exercise of governmental powers to create money, to tax, or to regulate the economy.

Clearly, there would be little or no purpose in examining the behaviour of any 'worst-case' government, if we accepted as prejudgement the notion that no external limits could possibly be effective in constraining the powers and authority granted. Given such a prejudgement, the best we might do would be to join the 'preachers' who try to convince politicians or officials that they should act 'morally'. Our whole approach, in this *Hobart Paper* and in earlier writings, is based on the presupposition that *constitutional constraints* on governmental behaviour can be effective, even if direct electoral controls are not.[1]

[1] For earlier works, James M. Buchanan and Gordon Tullock, *The Calculus of Consent*, University of Michigan Press, Ann Arbor, 1962; James M. Buchanan, *The Limits of Liberty*, University of Chicago Press, Chicago, 1975; James M. Buchanan, *Freedom in Constitutional Contract*, Texas A & M Press, College Station, 1978.

A more thorough analysis which provides the basis directly for that of this *Hobart Paper* is in Geoffrey Brennan and James M. Buchanan, *The Power to Tax: Analytical Foundations of a Fiscal Constitution*, Cambridge University Press, Cambridge, 1980, and notably Chapter VI for a specific and more detailed analysis of the money-creation power.

We assume the possible enforceability of constitutional checks and limits. Some analysis of the way that governments might be expected to behave under an explicit grant of money-issue power is then warranted. Quite apart from predictions on how governments might, in some average sense, use this power, to us it seems methodologically naïve to presume that governments, reflected in the actions of their agents, will behave benevolently rather than in accordance with their natural proclivities. Indeed, even as a predictive technique, 'natural government' seems superior to 'benevolent government'. This superiority is suggested by nothing more than a casual glance at the historical record, which clearly indicates that governments throughout the ages have tended to abuse the money-creation authority granted to them. Examples abound: Germany in the 1920s, Hungary in 1945-46, Britain in 1972-73, the United States in 1978-79, . . .

We shall use the term *monopoly government* to distinguish our basic conception from both *benevolent government*, which has dominated orthodox economic policy discussion, and *electorally-constrained government*, which has been reflected in 'public choice' literature.

Economic theory of monopoly applied to governmental monetary behaviour

We take the term 'monopoly' directly from economic theory, and much of the discussion involves rather straightforward application of the theory of monopoly in industry (Part II). Standard monopoly theory may be usefully compared with our extension to government. In economics, the monopolist is supposed always to exploit fully the profit potential of his entitlement or opportunity. Is this strictly how the individual monopolist behaves? Clearly not, since we may reckon that some monopolists may take into account the interests of potential customers, as well as much else. A monopolist may not choose to exploit fully the potential profit opportunity that his market power grants him. He may not behave strictly as wealth-maximising *homo economicus*, for any number of reasons: he may, for example, prefer the 'quiet life'.

Nonetheless, the theory of how the monopoly firm works is highly useful. It is properly conceived as an 'as if' theory that enables us to analyse conceptually the 'worst-case', to indicate the natural limits of consumers' vulnerability to exploitation, to define the maximal distortions in resource usage that monopoly can generate. And, on the basis of this theory, we can discuss the ways and means through which monopoly positions may be avoided and through which, if attained, they may be made short-lived.

The extension of this monopoly analysis to the government's use of its power to create money may be defended methodologically on precisely similar grounds. The theory of monopoly government, based on the notion that the monopoly powers will be exploited to the maximum, becomes a necessary ingredient to any constructive discussion of possible constitutional constraints. The theory need not be taken to imply that governments will always, or even on average, act as maximising monopolists. It does, nonetheless, allow us to set the limits to potential exploitation of the inherent or natural monopoly granted to government in money creation.

Specifically, we postulate that, if granted an unrestricted monopoly franchise to issue money, government will maximise the 'revenues' it can secure from this authority.[1] More correctly, and especially since the use of this power will cause inflation, the monopoly government will maximise its *real* revenues, its command over goods and services, the *real* value of the purchases it may make in the economy. In this setting, consider once again the first version of our fable of the little alchemist, which may now be extended to make the central point in this whole *Paper*. There will be natural limits on the amount of new gold he will want to make from sand, even if there is little or no cost. These limits will be set at the maximum value of real goods and services he can purchase with new gold.

By analysing government as a monolithic maximising entity, we are not, of course, suggesting that each and every person who participates in the very complex interaction of governmental decision processes devotes his or her energies solely to maximising real revenue for the government as a whole. Government, of course, is not a single entity. Our positive model is an abstract formulation that allows us to cut through the complexities of differential personal motivation and impose the unique 'maximand' as the objective. Again, some comparison with the orthodox theory of the monopoly firm becomes

---

[1] This revenue-maximisation objective in application to all forms of revenue-raising, and not limited to money creation, is central to the analysis in our book, *The Power to Tax, op. cit.*

relevant. A firm also makes decisions with the involved participation of many persons, who might have quite different personal motivations. But economists apparently find it illuminating to treat profits as the unique maximand. Our use of real revenues as the maximand for monopoly government is essentially identical.

Much of the following analysis, developed in some detail in Part II, is elementary. The critical threshold to be surmounted is the acceptance of the relevance and usefulness of the notion of monopoly in government behaviour. Once this threshold is crossed, the first version of our fable indicates that the central problem in inflation is the monopoly wielded by government in creating money.

PART II

Analysis: Unrestrained Government Monopoly In Creating Money

6. MONOPOLY FRANCHISES IN MONEY CREATION

The *status quo* provides ample empirical evidence that our whole exercise is grounded in reality. Most national governments in 1981 possess monopoly franchises in the creation of money, in one form or another. To our knowledge, no country allows a totally free market in money, and none limits the governmental rôle to the definition of value of a monetary unit in support of a pure commodity standard. Departures from strict monopoly franchises exist for a few small countries that tie their own currency values to that of larger currencies. Almost universally, national governments hold the authority to issue paper or fiat currency, either directly through governmental treasuries (as in Great Britain) or indirectly through governmentally-controlled central banks (as in Switzerland).

International influences on domestic money monopolist

National governments do not, of course, exist in total isolation, one from another, and the relationships among the separate national economies necessarily exert 'feedback' constraints on the domestic money-creation power. Most fundamentally, to the extent that citizens and corporations within a single country find it possible to hold balances, transact business, and make contracts designated in monies of other nations, the monopoly position of the home country government is weakened.

A truly international economy, in which citizens of all countries could deal in any one of many competing national monies, might seem to offer one means of substantially eliminating the monopoly power of any single national government.[1] But this 'solution' seems highly vulnerable as soon as we ask the simple question: Why would we expect any national government, now in possession of a money-creation monopoly franchise, to allow its citizens to make domestic transactions (in-

---

[1] This notion of competing monies seems to be roughly what Professor F. A. Hayek has in mind, although apparently he would also allow private citizens, in addition to governments, to issue money. (*Denationalisation of Money*, Hobart Paper 70, IEA, 1976; 2nd Edition, 1978.) Further discussion is in Part III.

cluding paying taxes) in the monies of other governments? Why would we expect any monopolist to allow its own profit opportunity to be eroded when it can exercise legal authority to prevent it? So long as national governments hold the legal power to define what shall be money for purposes of paying taxes, incurring debt obligations and making contracts, we must surely expect that this power will be used rather than abandoned. And this straightforward prediction is indirectly supported by the arguments of economists against competitive markets in money issue discussed in Part I.

In the analysis of Part II, we shall neglect the rôle that competitive constraints arising from the international economy might play in affecting the exploitation of the monopoly franchise in money. We do not, of course, deny that such constraints exist or that they are always insignificant. Even for a very large economy, the exchange value of its national currency relative to that issued by other countries will exert feedback influences on the issuing agent, even if we model the behaviour of this authority strictly in revenue-maximising terms. As in several other aspects of our analysis, however, we abstract from this feature. It seems prudent to put first things first. We shall model money-issue as if government is assigned a monopoly franchise in a *closed economy*. We leave it to others to modify the basic analysis as required to extend it as appropriate to an open economy.

7. TRANSACTIONS VALUE OF MONEY IN A NON-INFLATIONARY ECONOMY

Money performs a function of real value. It is not merely a veil. Persons will voluntarily exchange real goods and services for money units, even if they have no intrinsic worth and cannot be directly consumed or utilised. Money is valued for its instrumental usage in facilitating future exchanges. So long as people expect government either to accept money in payment of taxes or to give back real goods and services for money at a future date, government will be able to 'sell' pieces of paper designated 'money'. The real value of the money issue will be the *transactions* value that money serves in the economy.

Real capital value of monopolistic money issue

The government monopolist in money issue can secure this value even in a régime that is totally non-inflationary. Suppose society shifts abruptly from a pure barter to a money economy. The government simply issues a given nominal stock of money, M, as pieces of paper that will be used as media of exchange. Because of its value for transactions, individuals will 'purchase' this paper with goods and services, which the government will then have for its own use.

How much value in goods and services will people 'pay' for this money issue? What do they give up in each period in order to hold M units of money?—presumably real assets that could earn a rate of return, r, per period. The discounted value of the pieces of paper in the quantity, M, will, therefore, be $r.M/r$ or, simply, M. This real capital value of the money issue is independent of the quantity of nominal money issued by government. The same real value can be secured whether 1,000, 1,000,000, or 1,000,000,000 units (pieces of paper) are printed because the quantity issued will determine the level of prices for goods and services. And larger quantities of nominal units will have to be deflated by precisely corresponding larger price indices in order to compute the real value of the total issue. To say that the government captures real value, M, from its money issue we must therefore specify that M is designated in prices that will be set initially and which will prevail permanently since no additional money is to be issued.[1]

In this extremely rarified setting (the assumed non-inflationary régime), the government has no problem of making a choice. The government cannot issue more money in periods after the first, and, more importantly, people who 'purchase' the pieces of paper act as if they think there will be no government issue in later periods. In this setting, and under the assumed non-inflationary constraint, government is securing revenue from its monopoly power, but there is no maximising calculus. It will secure the full transactions value of money from *any* amount of issue.

---

[1] In this and the following sections we shall assume that the money monopolist captures the full potential value of the franchise. In régimes that involve fractional reserve banking by non-governmental firms, the monopolist may or may not be able to capture the full value: further discussed in Section 9.

If the monopoly monetary authority should, out of some motivation to 'do good', decide that it has no need or desire for the real revenue stemming from its franchise in money, it would have to do something to avoid making profits from its creation of money. It could proceed in either of two ways. It could pay all holders of money a rate of return, *r*, on their holdings, that it could presumably finance by general taxes on the citizenry. Or, alternatively, the government could define its pieces of paper so that the nominal number of units shrinks by the proportion *r* in each period, producing gradual deflation.

Under either procedure, the real capital value of the initial issue could be reduced to zero. In the first case, the holders of money receive the full transactions value of money in the economy, and without payment. The second procedure might possibly be arranged so that the holders of the nominal units of money would, in a sense, pay the taxes to subsidise themselves, which suggests that on equity grounds the second of the two methods might be preferred.[1]

8. REAL REVENUE POTENTIAL IN EXCESS OF TRANSACTIONS VALUE

Despite its usefulness in setting our analysis, we cannot simply *assume* a non-inflationary régime. And, as the discussion of the monopoly firm suggested (pp. 24-26), we do not propose to proceed as if governmental benevolence will produce non-inflationary monetary régimes. The preceding analysis was designed only to emphasise that real revenues may accrue from the possession of the money-creation franchise, even in the total absence of inflation. It was not intended to suggest that such a régime would emerge.

Such a prediction, given our concept of government as a maximiser of real revenue, could be made only if it could somehow demonstrate that the transactions value of money is

---

[1] Economist readers will recognise this scenario as that labelled as 'optimal' by Professor Milton Friedman. As our discussion perhaps suggests, the policy stance requires extremely naïve assumptions about the predicted behaviour of governments. Friedman was, of course, primarily concerned with the efficiency of the policy scenario, with efficiency defined in the strictest economic sense. (*The Optimum Quantity of Money and Other Essays*, Aldine, Chicago, 1969)

also the maximum value that the government could exact from the full exploitation of the monopoly money franchise. Such a proposition will not, in general, be valid, and the non-inflationary scenario would be approximated only under a very restrictive set of circumstances (pp. 30-31).

Full transactions value of money

In the non-inflationary régime, the holder of the franchise could secure the full transactions value of money in the economy independently of the quantity of nominal issue (p. 31).[1] If individuals expect that the size of the initial-period issue will remain permanently fixed, and that no further money creation will take place, and if they act on these expectations, the level of prices in the economy will adjust itself in direct proportion to the size of the nominal issue in the initial period. This relationship has often been stated in terms of the elasticity of demand for nominal money units, which remains at unity in the setting postulated; that is, a percentage increase in supply produces an exactly equal percentage decrease in demand.

In such a model the costs of holding a unit of money or cash is simply the rate of return that could be secured on an income-earning asset that could be purchased with that unit. For a single period, and setting the size of the unit at one, this cost is simply r.

How might the monopoly holder of the money-creation franchise extract more than the pure transactions value of money from citizens? It may do so by increasing the costs of holding cash balances above r, that is, by reducing the value of previously-issued nominal units of money by issuing new money in subsequent periods.

Suppose a person chooses to hold £1 in cash for one period when r is 10 per cent. The cost is 10 pence. He (or she) expects the £1 to possess the *same* capital value, by which we mean the same purchasing power over goods and services, at the end of the period as it had at the beginning. Suppose, however, that, during the period the initial-period money issue, M, is doubled,

---

[1] This proposition is nothing more than another version of the neo-classical theorem about the stability of the 'Cambridge k', the share of wealth that individuals want to hold as cash balances. So long as tastes do not change, and so long as expectations about the value of money are stable, they will want to hold the same share of their total assets in the form of cash.

and the holder of the £1 finds that prices have doubled. At the end of the period, the £1 will purchase only one-half the quantity of goods and services it could command at the start. The cost of holding the cash balance turns out to be 60 pence, as compared with 10 pence under the non-inflationary régime.

As this simple example suggests, the monopolist secures the pure transactions value of money in the economy, M, immediately on the initial issue. But more real value can be gained from the franchise by reducing the 'capital value' that persons have placed on money balances at the time they made decisions to hold cash. In the example, the 'capital value' of the £1 is reduced by one-half.

The limits to the monetary monopolist's real revenue

In the limit, the real revenue that the monopolist might gain may be much beyond that indicated in this example, given the state of expectations implicit in the analysis to this point. By issuing a sufficiently large quantity of nominal money in the second period, after people have made their decisions about holding cash balances based on the initial-period issue, the monopolist can reduce the capital values on the existing nominal units of money almost to zero.

Suppose that nominal units in the amount M are issued initially; people think this will be the fixed and permanent amount of nominal money in the economy and make plans accordingly. Suppose, now, the monetary authority issues 1,000 M in the second period. The holders of the initial M units of money will find the pieces of paper worth only 1/1,000 of what they expected when they made their initial decisions to hold cash.

The sequence may continue. Suppose that, with the 1,001 M in existence in the second period, people expect no subsequent money creation. They make plans to hold cash as before, but now the third period comes along and the monetary authority issues still more money in the amount of 1,000,000 M. In the limit, the monopolist may, at a maximum under this set of circumstances, secure the transactions value of money in the economy *in each and every period of time*, instead of only once, as in the non-inflationary régime. The monopolist is able to do this because he succeeds in wiping out the capital value of all previously existing money at the onset of each period. To the

[34]

individual the cost of holding £1 in cash for a single period approaches £1·10.[1]

9. BUT THE PEOPLE CANNOT BE FOOLED ALL THE TIME

This 'scenario' neglects an important constraint that will emerge to prevent such extreme exploitation of the monopolist's position. It is relevant only in the setting where all who make decisions to hold money balances do so in the continuing expectation that no additional money will be issued. In other words, people continue to hold the *same real value* of cash despite the continuing confiscation of the capital values of the cash they have held.

It is, of course, unrealistic to attribute such behaviour to all persons. The 'scenario' is, nonetheless, highly useful since it sets the extreme *upper limit* to the real revenue that a money-creation monopolist can gain from such a franchise. And so long as *anyone* acts in this way the gains to the government money-monopolist will include not only the transactions value of money but also the confiscations of the capital values in the cash held.

Analytical usefulness of assumption of individual rationality

But what if *all* individuals form their expectations 'rationally'? Modern-day economists are likely to shift all too readily to suppose that behaviour is at the opposite extreme from that argued here. They are likely to attribute rationality to everyone, as though all individuals act like highly trained economists. Nonetheless, working out the analysis under such extreme rationality assumptions is also useful for our purposes, because it should provide us with a lower limit to the present value of the money-creation franchise.

Suppose, now, that each person knows he (or she) confronts

---

[1] For the mathematically minded: the maximum present value, V, for the franchise in this model becomes:
$$V = M + M/(1+r) + M/(1+r)^2 \quad . \quad . \quad . \quad = \frac{M}{r}.$$

Hence, the present value of the monopoly franchise in this setting is $\frac{1}{r}$ times the value in the non-inflationary régime.

[35]

a revenue-maximising government monopolist of money issue. What sort of behaviour will be attributed to the monopolist? And how will decisions about holding cash be affected by such predictions about the monopolist's behaviour?

First, given any expectation of new money issues, a *lower real value* of wealth will be held in cash than otherwise. That is, the higher the costs of holding cash in real terms, the less will be held.

Second, and more complex, if the individual expects that the capital value of *any* cash balance he or she chooses to hold will be totally confiscated, or almost so, by inflationary issue of new currency, will it be rational to hold any balances at all? It seems likely that very few, and possibly none, of the individuals would hold money balances where they fully anticipated that their capital values would be almost totally wiped out by inflation. Ultimately, the economy would return to a barter régime. And although the monopolist holds the franchise to create money, none will then be accepted by citizens. The government will be unable to purchase goods and services with its pieces of paper labelled *Money*. The value of the monopoly franchise becomes zero.

10. THE CREDIBILITY DILEMMA

A dilemma thus exists if citizens are fully 'rational'. Individuals, as potential holders and users of money, find themselves unable to enjoy the genuine resource-saving economies that monetary transactions represent because of the anticipated prohibitive cost of holding cash. The resort to barter is grossly inefficient, but less so for the prospective holder than the anticipated confiscation of the capital value of balances. These potential holders and users of money would be willing to give up real goods for the services of money if, in some way, they could be insured against such confiscation.

At the same time, the governmental monopolist holding the money-creation franchise finds itself unable to exploit the potential profit that seems to exist. Since money creation, as such, is essentially costless, it would, of course, like to be able to purchase real goods and services with the pieces of paper, but it is prevented from so doing because people are unwilling to accept them.

Unexploited 'gains-from-trade'

There are unexploited 'gains-from-trade' as between the potential holders/users of money and the monetary authority. But, also, the agreement that might guarantee net benefits to both parties may be very difficult to negotiate due to the absence of effective enforcing mechanisms. There may be no means of negotiating a contract that both parties consider binding.

The monetary authority may seek to resolve the apparent *impasse* here by pre-announcement. It may announce a specific time-sequence for the issue of money over a whole set of periods. (Section 12 analyses the choice calculus of the monetary monopolist in selecting such a path of issue in the expectation that it will be binding and that the people so consider it.) But will individuals *believe* the pre-announcement and make their balance-holding plans accordingly? Will it be rational for them to do so?

Suppose the government issues M units of nominal money and announces that no more money will be issued. (This example could readily be modified to allow for any specific pre-announced rate of issue.) Suppose that everyone accepts the announcement in the belief that government is honest. They then shift the preferred share of their wealth into cash. It is evident that this capital value is ready for the taking by government should it choose to renege on its promise. By inflating the money issue beyond its commitment, government can confiscate almost the full capital value of any money balances previously accumulated. In so doing, of course, it will lose its credibility. People might believe such an announcement at one time, but having seen their capital confiscated through inflation subsequently, they are unlikely to be fooled again. Under what conditions will it be rational for the potential holder and user of money to anticipate that the government will renege?

11. THE DISCOUNT RATE FOR GOVERNMENT

If the government recognises in advance that it will lose credibility by reneging on its promise concerning future money issue, will it refrain from breaking such a promise? The answer clearly depends on the discount rate that describes the monopolist's behaviour.

Suppose the monopolist issues a quantity of nominal money initially, and promises that it will never issue additional quantities. If people believe the promise, government can secure the full present value of the money in the initial period, which it may either consume or invest in income-earning assets. If it invests in income-earning assets, the monopolist can collect an income in each period. But, in any subsequent period, it can, by a once-and-for-all inflation of issue (after which it may be able to secure no acceptance of new money), get approximately the full transactions value once again. If the discount rate is higher than the rate of return on investment, it seems evident that the rational government will renege on its commitment. If its discount rate is below the rate of return on investment, the government, even if it continues to act as a strict net revenue-maximiser, will rationally keep its word.

The monetary monopolist's rate of discount seems to depend on the ability to make portfolio adjustments, and on the anticipated permanence of the franchise.

Portfolio adjustment

For an individual, we do not ask what his private rate of discount is because we assume that he faces a market-determined rate to which portfolios are adjusted. Hence, at the appropriate margin of decision, the individual is always discounting at the market rate. It follows that he remains on the margin of indifference between continuing to hold a particular asset and cashing it in at market value and either consuming or re-investing the proceeds in alternative earning opportunities (transactions costs ignored). In application to the problem of choice that faces the monetary monopolist, the discount rate to which it adjusts itself would, indeed, be the market rate if it is able to adjust its portfolio like that of a private investor, and if its impact on the relevant market is small.

Since we are examining the behaviour of government as the holder of the money-creation franchise, it may seem far-fetched to discuss its portfolio adjustment as if it were a utility-maximising individual. There may be many types of institutional constraints that prevent such rational settling at the margins. We are analysing government as a revenue-maximising monopolist, but not necessarily assuming it is a unique choice-making entity. The complexities of political decision-making are well known, and, in themselves, they may prevent the fine tuning reflected in some ideally rationalised portfolio adjustment procedure.

In the real world, government may simply be unable to invest in earning assets, almost regardless of the form of political structure—whether democratic or autocratic. Pressures upon governmental decision-makers to use up all revenues collected for direct consumption may be so strong as to forestall any accumulation of earning assets, quite independently of the discount rate preferred by the decision-makers. Even if, in one sense, this rate should be very low, or even zero, the investment-capital accumulation rules indicated by the simple relationship between such an internal rate and the rate of return on assets may not be carried out because of internal constraints in the political process itself (such as prohibitions on government investment in private securities).

Further than this, government may not find itself able to accumulate non-earning assets in any liquid form; hoarding as well as investment may be impossible. Government may be forced to spend all funds it has within single budget periods. Even if it cannot make portfolio adjustments like an individual, however, its rate of discount may still be such as to cause it to hold back from seeking confiscation of all the potential value of existing cash held by the public.

The permanence of the franchise

By all odds the most important element affecting the discount rate will be the anticipated length of the revenue franchise, whether for money-creation or other forms of revenue-raising. If government considers itself permanently entrenched, with no prospect of replacement or revolution, its decision-makers may take the long view, which would, of course, indicate a low rate of discount for the time-sequence of money-issue. (The same conclusion could be reached for all forms of taxation of capital.) The short-term prospects of getting real revenue by

[39]

departing from any pre-announced path of money issue might be fully recognised, and the desirability of securing the goods that such revenues might purchase may remain intense, but government that thinks itself permanent will also recognise the long-term costs that loss of credibility would generate. The behaviour of a permanent monopoly government may, therefore, approach that of a government that finds itself externally constrained (either by moral precepts or constitutional law) to live by its commitments.

The continuing strain of such a behavioural sequence should, however, be reckoned with. The prospects for short-term gains do not evaporate with one exercise of discipline; they continue to entice government in each and every period. And if and when government that has considered itself permanently installed in power modifies its perspective and sees a possible end to its franchise, the potential attractiveness of capital-value confiscation through inflation may come to dominate its behaviour.

Even with a permanent monopoly franchise, therefore, the citizens who make money-balance choices in the expectation that government promises will be honoured are taking a precarious leap of faith. If we shift attention to what we may call a 'temporary' franchise, the prospects for departures from monetary commitments are much higher. The government that sees itself in office or in power only for a fixed period will not reckon on the costs in loss of credibility during subsequent periods. It will have every incentive to inflate the money issue during the closing years of its reign, since it thus can confiscate the capital values represented in money balances at very little cost to itself.

Incentive to inflation of 'temporary' democratic government
The implications for the much-justified rotation of democratically-elected governmental régimes are evident even if surprising. A government that knows itself to be a temporary holder of an effective monopoly franchise in money-creation will have every incentive to generate very substantial inflation during its terminal years. Given the same basic motivation for each of two governments, a continuing rotation in office of the two would be predicted to exploit the monopoly prospects of the money-creation franchise more fully than if either one of the two were placed in permanent office. In democratic electorates,

[40]

the prospects for re-election and of citizens' historical memories of performances by governments will temper somewhat these seemingly paradoxical conclusions but not the direction of effect.

Our central subject is a revenue-maximising government. But suppose it maximises revenue only some of the time? Instead of the extreme assumption that all governments all the time behave as if they seek to secure the maximum gains from their monopoly franchise, let us assume that 'good' governments may exist, but that there remains always a probability that they will take on the revenue-maximising rôle. Suppose, for example, that an individual estimates that one government in three will act more or less as the maximiser of monopoly gains, and that it will use the money-issue franchise to maximise its command over real goods and services. The 'good' government that refrains from exploiting the monopoly potential of the franchise may then be of little or no value to the citizen. If he makes money-balance decisions on the basis of the observed behaviour of a 'good' government (behaviour that keeps money-issue in pre-commitment limits), he will be offering enhanced opportunities for the monopoly revenue-maximiser when and if it finally emerges in the political process. The citizen might be better off to remain highly cynical and to adjust his money-balance behaviour on the presumption that the revenue-maximising government *exists even when it does not.*

12. REVENUE-MAXIMISING INFLATION WHEN COMMITMENTS ARE HONOURED AND WHEN INDIVIDUALS EXPECT THEM TO BE HONOURED

The analysis so far has suggested some of the difficulties that emerge in an attempt to define an individual's rational response in confrontation with a revenue-maximising monetary authority. We shall return to this central problem in Section 13. What of the behaviour of the revenue-maximising monopolist and of the individual on the presumption that any government undertaking to a money-issue sequence will be honoured, and that the individual acts as if he expects such government behaviour? What would the revenue-maximising calculus of the monetary authority be under this self-imposed constraint? What rate of inflation will it select?

[41]

This question has, perhaps surprisingly, been analysed relatively completely in the economics literature,[1] whereas most of the other questions raised in this *Hobart Paper* have been almost totally neglected, although they seem equally, if not more, important. The reason for this rather disproportionate treatment is attributable, at least in part, to the presumption that the analysis is more generally applicable than our structure suggests.

The costs to individuals of holding cash

The share of wealth an individual chooses to hold in the form of money balances will be related to the costs of holding them. The higher such costs are expected to be, the lower the real value of wealth that will be held in cash. The costs of holding cash balances are composed of two elements: the interest that the money holder could earn if he held his assets in the form of bonds or other non-money wealth rather than cash; and the reduction in the real value of his cash holdings that is associated with general inflation. (This latter 'cost' could, in principle, be a benefit if the government were to deflate so that the real value of cash rose over time.) The larger such 'costs', the smaller the cash balances people will hold, but the larger the revenue government can obtain from each £1 held. There will be some rate of inflation (new currency issue) that will maximise the total value to government of the money-issue franchise: applying that rate secures for government, in total, more real goods than the simple non-inflationary régime. This remains true even if the rate of inflation is announced in advance, if the monopolist lives by its promises, and if individuals believe it will do so. Or, in other words, even if the rate of inflation is fully anticipated by all potential holders of money, there will remain an incentive for government to select an inflationary rather than a non-inflationary régime.[2]

---

[1] For example, Martin Bailey, 'The Welfare Costs of Inflationary Finance', *Journal of Political Economy* 64, April 1956, pp. 93-110; Edward Tower, 'More on the Welfare Cost of Inflationary Finance', *Journal of Money, Credit and Banking*, 9, November 1971, pp. 850-860.

[2] For economists among our readers we can be somewhat more technical.

The demand for real balances falls as the costs rise. One point on the demand curve is that which is represented by the non-inflationary régime, where there is some initial quantity of money issued, M, along with the authority announcement that no subsequent issue will be forthcoming. (For analytical convenience

[*Continued on page 43*]

[*Continued from page 42*]

here, we shall assume a no-growth economy. In an economy with real growth, new money may be issued proportionately to such growth while keeping prices stable.)

In the non-inflationary régime, the government gains the pure transactions value of money, M, but nothing more. It should perhaps be clear that this arrangement need not, and presumably will not, be that which maximises the present value of the franchise. The monetary authority will try instead to select precisely that rate of money emission (and inflation) through time that will maximise present value, given the presumed constraint that it must pre-announce the rate of emission in all subsequent periods and stick to its promises.

Differing rates of continuing and permanent inflation can be represented as different points along the demand curve for real balances, this time drawn for the whole community (see Figure 1). The revenue-maximising position will be located where the elasticity of this curve is unitary. The rectangle subtended under the demand curve will measure present value of the franchise. We should note that, in this arrangement, the authority cannot gain as much real value in the initial period as it could under the non-inflationary régime. This result emerges because, with any positive rate of inflation that is fully anticipated, individuals will not use real goods to 'purchase' as much in real money balances as they would do under the non-inflationary régime.

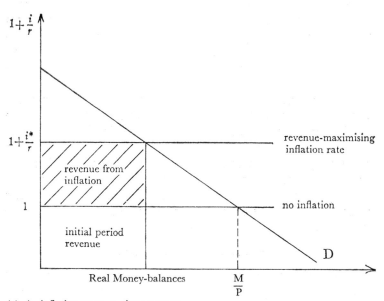

(a) i=inflation rate; r=interest rate.
(b) D is the transactions demand for money.

Figure 1

Nonetheless, the present value of the franchise is higher under anticipated inflation than without because the present value of the anticipated and announced rate of confiscation of capital values in real balances must be added on over and above the transactions value of the issue that can be gained in the first period.

13. THE GREAT MONETARY GAME

Some contributors to the orthodox discussion of this question examined the histories of great inflations in several countries and expressed some surprise that governments seem to have allowed (caused) rates of inflation far *exceeding* any plausibly-computed revenue-maximising limits, given the fully-anticipated, fully-announced models of analysis. Why?

If government is studied as a monopoly, these results are not at all surprising. Indeed, our construction allows us to trace out a sequence. Government may decide to finance a portion of its future outlays by inflation, and announce its intention to generate a fixed rate of emission, with the initial purpose of living up to the commitment. As it issues the new money, however, it finds that it has severely over-estimated the quantity of real goods and services that can be financed by this method. Why are its estimates always likely to err in this direction? Because, quite simply, *individuals do not really expect governments to live by their promises,* and, therefore, hold *less* real balances than the amount projected for them by government. Government then finds it necessary to inflate the money supply *more* than it had projected in order to finance its spending commitments.

This *'strategic'* aspect of the interaction between government and individuals in money creation cannot, and should not, be overlooked or assumed non-existent. And rules for what is and what is not rational behaviour in such situations are not universally agreed upon. We have emphasised earlier the *impasse* between government and potential cash holders, and the difficulties of negotiating enforceable agreements. Another critical aspect of the money creation game now deserves some attention.

The monetary game is 'unfair'

The 'game' between the monetary authority and individuals is biased in favour of the government monopolist because of the elementary fact that individuals must make money-balance choices before the money-issue choices made by government in subsequent periods. It is as if one player in a game, the money franchise holder, is always allowed to 'go last' after the other player has made his commitment. It is hardly a 'fair' game.

It is this feature of the great monetary game—individuals

must play first—that allows for the substantial degree of exploitation of the monopoly position. Individuals are not allowed to adjust their behaviour after they know what government is going to do about the money issue or even simultaneously with government's action. They are not allowed to react merely to an announcement, as they are normally allowed to do with an ordinary tax.

Tax on beer contrasted with 'tax' on money

Consider a tax on beer. Suppose government has been allowed to tax beer, which is equivalent to giving it a monopoly franchise in the sale of beer.[1] Individuals can adjust their behaviour in response to the tax-induced price increase; they can switch to wine without suffering substantial capital value losses over and above the amount they will pay in tax on the beer they choose to continue to purchase.

Contrast this sequence with the 'tax' on money that inflation represents. Individuals have made decisions to hold balances. Someone must continue to hold all the units of money in existence. There is no escape: the money previously issued must be held by somebody. Individuals may, and will, of course, choose to reduce the value of their money balances once they see that government is issuing new money. But the only way of accomplishing this result is to bid up money prices for goods. Hence, persons who hold money must suffer, necessarily, substantial capital losses on all previously held money balances.

It is in this sense that the inflation 'tax' on money balances is *retroactive*. It is this feature that makes such a 'tax' more closely analogous to a tax on capital assets than to a tax on any income or expenditure base. Individuals must make decisions to accumulate capital through time, and capital cannot be consumed immediately, once it has been accumulated. Hence, a tax on capital that is not anticipated long in advance can effectively confiscate capital values. Such a tax can yield revenues of more than 100 per cent of the income from the capital assets that are taxed. By comparison, 100 per cent of income is the absolute maximum revenue limit under an income tax.

What then is 'rational expectation' in the great monetary

---

[1] *The Power to Tax, op. cit.*, elaborates this and related arguments.

game between the monetary monopolist and individuals?[1] The upper limit on the monopolist's gain is set when all individuals continue to believe in every period that government has made its last issue of money. The lower limit is zero, when all individuals fully anticipate that the monopolist will move immediately to confiscate the full capital values of all real money balances and hence hold no balances in the form of money at all. For individuals, as potential holders and users of money, the upper limit on the benefits is the full transactions value in a non-inflationary régime, for which they would stand ready and willing to hand over to the monopolist.[2] The lower limit is the possibly very significant capital value confiscation that would emerge if individuals continued to act as if they believed the monopolist's pronouncements independently of its observed behaviour.

People learn to offset the actions of the inflationary monetary monopolist: towards a contractual approach?

The game is played between these limits. It seems plausible to suggest that different individuals in the economy will react differently. Some will presumably continue to be fooled for long periods; they will continue to add to and to hold real money balances in the face of continuing confiscation of values by inflation. The great hyperinflations in Hungary, Germany and other countries corroborate this statement.[3] To the extent that some individuals behave in this fashion, the monopolist has an enhanced incentive to inflate, despite the loss of value its behaviour may impose on persons who anticipate its action more accurately.

Through time, of course, as more and more people go through the learning process and come to predict the monetary issue policy of the government accurately, and as the real revenue gains from inflation approach zero, the incentive for

---

[1] One of the few examinations of the strategic aspects of the interaction between government and individuals is contained in Andrew Schatter and Gerald O'Driscoll, 'Why Rational Expectations May Be Impossible: An Application of Newcomb's Paradox', Discussion Paper, Center for Applied Economics, New York University, November 1978.

[2] We neglect the 'welfare triangle' that represents the added value that might be secured from a deflationary rate that just offsets the rate of return on real assets.

[3] Philip Cagan, 'The Monetary Dynamics of Hyperinflation', in Milton Friedman (ed.), *Studies in the Quantity of Money*, University of Chicago Press, Chicago, 1956, pp. 25-117.

government (as well as for individuals) to seek ways and means of devising some sort of enforceable agreement or contract to avoid the dilemma of the monetary game is increased.

14. MONETARY MONOPOLY AND DEPOSIT BANKING

Our analysis is based in the presumption that the government monopolist with the money-creation franchise is able to capture all the potential value ('monopoly rent') of such a franchise. In terms of a simple institutional structure, the analysis applies to an economy where the only monetary unit is the fiat currency (usually paper with no inherent value) issued by the governmental authority. In reality, such economies are rare. In most modern countries, fiat currency makes up only a part of the effective money in the economy. Fiat issue serves as a high-powered base for the derivative issue of bank money in the form of deposits. Can the analysis be applied to a monetary system that includes deposit banking as well as government fiat issue?

No difficulty arises if we suppose that the monetary monopoly sells the banking franchise to a single private firm in some sort of competitive auction process. The government would then capture the full value of all money issued just as if all the money were fiat. The analysis holds without qualification.

Can monopoly of money work with a competitive deposit banking system?

Problems seem to arise in competitive banking. How can the governmental monopolist then secure the potential value from bank-money creation? And, if it cannot do so, why should the governmental monopolist ever allow fractional-reserve banking to persist in which banks may create deposits in a stated multiple of reserves (as in the USA).

The introduction of fully competitive fractional-reserve deposit banking does not modify the real-revenue potential available to the fiat-issue governmental monopolist. Some share of the transactions value of money in the system will be returned to individuals as payment for their holding bank deposits. The opportunity cost (the yield on investments foregone) of holding money balances will be lower than under a régime in which no interest is paid on deposits. The public will hold more value in cash, for any given rate of inflation, than it will in a pure currency system. This difference allows the fiat-issue monopolist to generate a higher real-revene maximising rate of inflation than under a pure fiat system. In effect, to the extent that fractional-reserve banking is competitive, our earlier analysis holds without qualification.

Reserve ratio control gives power to impose capital levies on banks

Fractional-reserve banking does, however, provide the monopoly government with one additional instrument of control. If it is legally authorised to change the required reserve ratio, the governmental monetary monopolist may be able to use this authority to impose what amounts to a capital levy on deposit holders (as in unexpected inflation, p. 49), without changing the rate of inflation.

If deposit banking is neither explicitly monopolistic nor fully competitive, if free entry into banking is not allowed, as it is not in many countries, banking charters or licences will, of course, be valuable, and, directly or indirectly, government can require payment for them.

15. MONEY CREATION, PUBLIC DEBT AND INCOME TAXES

So far, we have talked as if the sole effect of inflation on government revenue occurs through the financing of deficits by the creation of new money. This is an important and obvious aspect of inflation as a revenue device. But there are two other effects of inflation, both relevant for total government revenue yields and obligations.

The first is the effect of 'unexpected' inflation on the government's liabilities to service and redeem its interest-bearing debt. The second is the effect of inflation on personal income tax revenues. The significance of these less direct aspects of the revenue-implications of inflation may be, in total, at least as large in real terms as the matters that have been the focus of interest here.

[48]

All debtors, including government, benefit from unexpected inflation
Consider the effect on interest-bearing debt. Suppose the government has borrowed from private citizens an amount representing outstanding liabilities with a present value of, say, one million pounds in original prices. A once-and-for-all increase, say a doubling, in the money supply, totally unexpected but not expected to be repeated, will cause a reduction in the real liabilities represented by outstanding debt issue of half the total liability—half a million pounds in original prices. The reason is clear. Unexpected inflation redistributes real resources away from lenders to borrowers when all liabilities are specified in money values. To the extent that the government is a net borrower, it will gain when unexpected inflation occurs. In the example considered here, there will be no effect of the price increase on nominal interest rates because the increase in the money supply is not expected to be repeated.

If, on the other hand, the government made a once-and-for-all move from one 'permanent' inflationary régime to another, it would have to raise the nominal interest rate on all future debt issue. If the nominal interest rate rises so as to maintain the real rate (the nominal rate minus the rate of inflation, roughly), there would be no revenue advantage to government except in the period between régimes, which we take to be unexpected.

Therefore, except where government debt is indexed so that its real value to the private lenders is maintained despite inflation, essentially the same possibilities for revenue acquisition by government arise with interest-bearing debt as with non-interest bearing cash. The analysis of the effects of new money creation on the real wealth of holders of cash can be extended to include the real wealth of holders of government debt. The effect of inflation is to redistribute wealth from *both* private groups to government.

Inflation raises real government revenue from progressive income tax
The effects of inflation on the real value of income tax revenue are clear. The interaction of inflation with a progressive income tax rate structure increases *real* government revenue: inflation forces taxpayers into higher tax brackets and raises the average rate of tax for virtually everyone. (The exception is the group of taxpayers who after the inflation remain in the lowest tax bracket.)

[49]

This effect, although of considerable revenue significance, is quite different in its manner of operation from the effects of inflation on debt and cash holders. The taxpayer can, if he chooses, adjust his work and earnings *currently* to higher income tax rates, whether induced through inflation or discretionary legislative action; he can change jobs, refuse to work overtime, or refrain from seeking promotion to more arduous responsibilities, in response to higher effective income tax rates. He cannot so react if he is holding cash or government debt. In this sense, there is an important element of retroactivity in holding money-debt that is absent in paying income tax.

It is this element of retroactivity that renders the citizenry particularly vulnerable to exploitation *via* inflation, and that has consequently been the focus of our discussion here. It is this incapacity of the private citizen to avoid the oppressive monetary power of government that creates a case for a *monetary* constitution, even where explicit restrictions on income tax rates (or total tax revenues) are not considered desirable to enable him to avoid the oppressive fiscal power of government.

Part III

The Implications for Policy

16. THE 'ILLEGITIMACY' OF UNCONSTRAINED MONETARY MONOPOLY

National governments' monopoly franchises in money creation are not normally constrained in any specific way. The analysis of Part II, building on the political models developed in Part I, offers convincing arguments that such unconstrained monopoly franchises are *illegitimate*, and that they should be recognised as such.

Having made this statement, we must define 'illegitimacy' and, by inference, 'legitimacy' quite carefully.[1] When we state that unconstrained monopoly franchises in money creation are 'illegitimate', we are implying that such monetary arrangements could not be derived as a legally-justifiable part of the basic 'laws of the land', that is, of the constitutional order of a society. To justify such a statement, we must say what we mean by 'legally justifiable'.

Criteria for evaluating basic social/economic institutions

What are the ultimate criteria for evaluating the basic institutions of a desirable social order? If we reject the existence of (or at least general agreement on) external ethical norms such as those sometimes claimed to be present in 'natural law' or 'revealed religion', the criteria for evaluation of institutions must in some way be *derived from individuals themselves* as the only conscious, evaluating beings.

Individuals have their own identifiable interests, which may differ sharply among separate persons, families, groups, and social classes. How, then, can any generally applicable criteria be derived that will succeed in cutting through the conflicts among private or individual interests?

---

[1] Our use of the terms 'legitimacy' and 'illegitimacy' may be unfamiliar to economists, but they will be recognised by political scientists and political philosophers who have discussed the 'legitimacy' and 'illegitimacy' of political institutions and of government for centuries. We have deliberately chosen to use these terms rather than milder ones such as 'acceptability' and 'unacceptability' because our application to the monetary arrangements of society is precisely analogous to the broader application to government generally.

[53]

One means lies in removing the identification that the individual can make concerning his interest. If a person does not know either who he will be or, somewhat more realistically, how a particular legal institution will affect his interest, he will evaluate institutions in general terms instead of individualised interest.[1] Institutions or rules will tend to be selected so as to satisfy what has sometimes been called 'fairness' standards.

Viewed in this light, an institution stands the test of 'legitimacy' if it can be demonstrated that it could have been, or could possibly be, *agreed* on by all persons each of whom remains unable to identify the direct impact of that institution on his private interest. The contractual agreement that might be attained, or might have been attained, either behind the genuine Rawlsian 'veil of ignorance' or under the Buchanan/Tullock conditions of extreme uncertainty about the impact of institutions on individual interests, allows us to classify 'legitimate' and 'illegitimate' institutions for social order, including monetary arrangements.[2]

Voluntary agreement for unconstrained monetary monopoly would be impossible

The thrust of our argument is negative rather than positive. We claim that unconstrained government monopoly in money creation cannot emerge from a genuine constitutional calculus in which everyone participates and where individual positions are not identifiable or predictable. There may be several alternative monetary arrangements about which such a negative conclusion could not be reached, such as a commodity standard, a system of competitive monies, or fiat issue under

---

[1] The evaluative procedure described briefly here, where the individual literally *does not know* who he will be, is a summary of the Rawlsian 'veil of ignorance' construction. (John Rawls, *A Theory of Justice*, Harvard University Press, Cambridge, Mass., 1971.) A less restrictive variant, where the individual may be able to identify himself but *cannot predict* how a particular institution will affect his interest, is developed in James M. Buchanan and Gordon Tullock, *The Calculus of Consent*, University of Michigan Press, Ann Arbor, 1962.

[2] By suggesting that monopoly franchises in money creation are 'illegimate', we are claiming basically that such arrangements could never have been, and could never be, agreed to *volunatrily* in a genuine social contract. In using such a 'contractarian' criterion for classification we are not, of course, implying that a genuine 'social contract' took place in history, or indeed that one could now take place. We claim only that the conceptual device of such a contract is used as a criterion for determining the possible acceptability of existing or proposed institutions or rules.

[54]

constitutional constraints (several of these will be further discussed in Section 19). Any one of them may be preferred to unconstrained monopoly franchise, and we do not try to argue for any one from the many possible constitutionally-acceptable alternatives. But progress in discussion will have been made if we can first secure agreement on what is *not* acceptable.

17. LEGALLY-PROTECTED AND UNCONSTRAINED MONOPOLY IN PRODUCTION OR SALE

The argument may be generalised as well as exemplified by reference to any good or service that yields value in the economy, say, cornflakes (or milk, or apples). Suppose that an unconstrained but legally protected monopoly in the production and sale of cornflakes (or milk, or apples . . .) should be proposed as an integral part of the institutional arrangements for society, and that this sort of proposal is taken under consideration at an initial stage of constitutional deliberation.

In the setting postulated for individual evaluation, individuals could not predict what their own positions might be on cornflakes. They will have no idea whether or not they might turn out to be consumers of cornflakes, owners of labour or capital used in the production and distribution of cornflakes, or recipients of the possible rents or profits that the holders of the cornflake franchise can expect to secure. They know only that the proposal before them involves the assignment of the rights to production and sale of cornflakes to a single individual or firm in the economy, that there will be no constraints on behaviour of the franchise-holder, and that the forces of the state will prevent the entry of potential competitors into the production and sale of cornflakes . . .

Unregulated legal monopoly causes net social welfare loss

The first term in elementary economics is sufficient to suggest that ordinary people would never voluntarily agree to such an arrangement for monopolisation of the production and sale of cornflakes. They would reckon on the net welfare or efficiency loss that any such legally protected but unregulated monopoly franchise would generate, a net loss to the community that

[55]

they would reckon on sharing, at least in part, since their individual position on cornflakes remains unidentified.

We can, of course, replace cornflakes (or milk, or apples) in all the above discussion by 'money', except for one important difference: there are far more opportunities for exploitation in a money-creation monopoly than there are with common-or-garden goods and services. In a real sense, money balances take the form of a capital good for which there is *no close substitute* in an economy: it is a 'natural' monopoly of a peculiar sort.

Natural monopoly and legal enforcement

But what about a standard 'natural monopoly'? Suppose our designated commodity, cornflakes . . ., can be produced with economies of large-scale production.[1] The 'natural' forces of market competition would then evolve towards the domination of the whole cornflakes industry by a single firm, which would have an effective monopoly. If this tendency is recognised in advance, is there not an argument for legal monopoly, with the franchise granted through some device to the firm that might best qualify (through auction or otherwise)?

It is necessary to be clear on what such a grant of legal monopoly means. If it refers to governmental enforcement and protection against competitive entry of new firms into the industry, even when 'natural monopoly' exists, no such grant of legal monopoly can be justified unless it is accompanied by one that suggests simultaneous *enforceable limits or restraints* on the exercise of the sheltered monopolist's power. No argument for *unrestrained* legal monopoly is to be found even in the most naïvely-based support for special rights of 'natural monopolies'.

Two separate types of constraint on potential monopolistic behaviour must be distinguished.

First, potential or actual entry of competitors into an industry represents a restraint that is always present regardless of the dominating position of a firm *so long as there are no effective barriers to entry* enforced by government.

Second, if such barriers exist and potential entry exerts no restraint on behaviour, *regulation* may be designed to temper the degree of exploitation of the monopoly opportunity. The

---

[1] We are not concerned here with the validity of the hypothesis that such 'production functions' exist. We concentrate on the implications of the hypothesis 'as if' it were valid.

history of government intervention into the affairs of business allegedly designed to serve the 'public interest', such as in fuel and transport, education and health, provides ample evidence that all such businesses must accept the imposition of regulatory constraints in exchange for the grant of monopoly privilege.

18. WHY HAS MONEY BEEN TREATED DIFFERENTLY?

'Natural monopoly' is one form of the 'market failure' argument. We have discussed the general 'market failure' arguments made by economists with reference to monetary arrangements (pp. 16-18). These arguments have been used to justify not only a governmental rôle in money matters, but also, and almost inadvertently, they have been extended to support the assignment of a *monopoly* right to create money by an agency or authority of government. We have suggested (pp. 19-21) there is no *prima facie* case for governmental intervention even if 'market failure' against some ideal is demonstrated. But our emphasis here is that, even if we provisionally accept some such justification, it cannot possibly extend to any support of the assignment of *unrestrained* monopoly power.

Economists have been uncritical of government monopoly in money

The very existence of monopoly franchises in money creation, which seem virtually free of explicit retraining rules, thus seems anomalous. Even stranger, perhaps, has been the relative paucity of economists' criticism of such institutional arrangements. Why has money somehow been assigned this special place?

We offer no fully satisfactory answer. The best we can do is our discussion of the benevolent-despot blindness that has created confusion among economists in their consideration of policy for a century. If the economist commences his task with the implicit presumption that governmental arms and agencies will at least try to 'do good', he will necessarily reject out of hand *any* enforceable constraint on governmental behaviour. He will, indeed, object (possibly strongly) to our whole monopoly construction in this *Hobart Paper* and elsewhere, whether we apply it to a monetary monopoly or to other governmental agencies. To such economists, there is really no meaning in efforts to define the limits to the exploitation of the monopolist's position, if the monopolist is benevolent by presupposition.

Even within the limits of the benevolent despot presumption, something seems amiss. There are many ways of 'doing good', and different political leaders motivated exclusively by their own interpretation of the 'public interest' will define their objectives differently. For many of these politicians, 'doing good' comes down to the spending of public monies. Hence, even for the most benevolent of politicians, revenue becomes a goal to maximise, an instrument through which they can promote public happiness and well-being. Would it not then follow that, for such well-meaning politicians, revenue-*increasing* policy is to be preferred to revenue-*decreasing* policy? Would it not follow that, for such agents, inflation might still offer a very tempting source of gains?

Our brief and temporary acceptance of the heroic prospect that politicians may wish to promote the 'public interest' in their own lights, is perhaps sufficient to suggest that the argument against *unconstrained* grant of monopoly powers to any governmental agency of money issue does not critically depend on our extreme formulation of the revenue-maximising monopolist. It is, however, helpful in exposing 'natural' tendencies within government that can be disciplined by institutional-constitutional arrangements.

19. MONETARY ARRANGEMENTS TO MEET CONSTITUTIONAL TESTS

We have suggested that there may exist several institutional structures for ordering the monetary affairs of a community, any one of which may possibly qualify under our contractarian-constitutional test for acceptability. It may be conceptually possible for individuals to agree upon any one of such arrangements, which would then discipline unconstrained monetary monopoly. We do not propose to 'take sides' and to advance an argument in support of any of the arrangements that might meet the constitutional-agreement test. We present the alternatives and discuss each in summary to contrast the predicted working properties with those of unconstrained monopoly.

There are four régimes to be considered:

(1) *Free market in money, with no governmental role*

If unconstrained monetary monopoly is rejected as constitutionally unacceptable, there emerges essentially a two-stage question. Should government be assigned *any* rôle in ordering monetary affairs? And, if so, how should the powers be constrained?

Given adverse predictions about the operation of government in any rôle that might be assigned to it in running the supply of money, a constitutional evaluation may possibly suggest that the more desirable arrangement would be a totally free market in money, with no direct money-creating governmental rôle at all. The legal-political-governmental setting would require to be specified carefully, even here. We must presume that the government would be limited to minimal or protective state functions, largely involved in enforcing property rights and contracts among private parties.

There would then be no direct governmental rôle in money at all. The government would not define the medium of exchange; it would not print money; it would not regulate private printing of money or bank notes; it would not regulate banking or credit. Money would emerge, but exclusively as private money (or monies), with no government guarantees or repurchase arrangements. Government could, presumably, choose to collect taxes in the money or monies of its choice, just as private individuals might choose to make contracts in the money or monies of *their* choice.

Behaviour of government money monopolist crucial to choice between it and free markets in money

We earlier (pp. 17-18) sketched out economists' arguments that such free-market arrangements in money would tend to embody over-expansions and over-contractions. We are persuaded that these arguments, generally, are valid, and only a minority of economists would disagree. But even if we fully accept the 'market failure' analysis of free markets in money, they may be preferred to an unrestrained government monopoly.

[59]

The choice depends, in part, on a judgement of how the governmental authority would behave. If it is predicted that *any* assignment of a monetary rôle to government must inevitably degenerate into the unconstrained monopoly of money issue, the free-market argument becomes highly persuasive. It would amount to ruling out all the three other succeeding régimes as impracticable or implausible, although accepting that some initial constitutional prohibition would keep government totally out of the monetary picture.

(2) *Governmental money issue, but competitive entry*

A second régime that warrants examination is that which Professor Hayek seems to have in mind in his proposal for competitive monies. We could not expect any government already possessed of a monopoly power to introduce and adhere to a régime that allows free entry into money creation. But we should consider the Hayek proposal seriously as a constitutionally-selected set of monetary arrangements to guarantee such competitive entry.

In such a set of institutions, government may be empowered to issue domestic money, in whatever quantities it may choose. In this sense it would possess a monopoly franchise and it may be totally unrestrained in size of issue. The restraints present here, however, would emerge from the guarantee of free entry. The constitution would guarantee that individuals could hold balances, make private contracts, including the incurring of debts, and conduct ordinary transactions in any money of their choosing. This would open up the prospects for free entry, and citizens could use monies issued by foreign governments, commodity monies such as gold, or even paper monies issued by private firms and banks. The forces of competition would act as the restraint on the government money-issue monopoly, and if this agency attempted to exploit the profit potential of its position through inflation, its own money issue would quickly lose value.

The possible advantage of this set of arrangements over the totally free-market alternative lies in its incentives and sanctions for the government-issue monopolist to remain within non-inflationary bounds, whilst also offering some protection against the waves of expansion and contraction the free market might generate. The monopolist might recognise the potential for securing the transactions value of money in the economy, and individuals might also recognise the incentives for the monopolist to stay within pre-announcement limits.

(3) *Pure commodity money, with governmental definition of value*
A third set of monetary institutions, various schemes for commodity or commodity-based money, is more familiar. The governmental rôle is limited to the definition of the monetary value of a physical unit of a designated commodity (or bundle of commodities in specified proportions). An ounce of gold of a specified degree of fineness is defined to be of, say, $400 in value, and the government 'opens its window' to sell and to purchase gold at this price. It does not create money on its own account; and if there is paper money it is convertible at a fixed price directly into the base commodity at the governmental money window.

The advantage of this arrangement is that the incentives of the profit-and-loss system are harnessed to generate stability rather than instability in the value of the monetary unit. If general price levels rise, while the value of the monetary commodity remains fixed, resources used in producing the money commodity become unprofitable; the rate of production falls, and the supply of money grows less rapidly, dampening the inflation in prices. On the other hand, if prices of non-money commodities fall, production of the money commodity becomes more profitable, leading to an expansion in the supply of money.[1]

The disadvantages of this set of institutions are twofold. First, the quantity of money is dependent on the elasticity of supply of the gold or other monetary commodity, and if this elasticity is low, there may be damaging lags in the working of the competitive forces.

Second, and perhaps much more importantly, any commodity-based monetary system tends to degenerate into a combination of an unrestrained government monopoly and an unrestrained free market in money. The goldsmith scenario (pp. 15-16) becomes directly relevant. Any pure commodity standard tends to become a commodity *reserve* standard, with potential profits to be exploited both by government and by

---

[1] A general discussion of alternative constitutional money arrangements, with special discussions of commodity standards, is in Leland B. Yeager (ed.), *In Search of a Monetary Constitution*, Harvard University Press, Cambridge, Mass., 1962.

private firms. Units of the money commodity, as such, would be used as reserves upon which derivative or 'low-powered' paper money would be issued. To police a commodity standard effectively, and to prevent such conversion into reserve usage of the money commodity, much governmental regulation over and above the mere definition of the value of the monetary unit would have to be laid down in the constitution.

(4) *Fiat money issue constrained by constitutional rules*

Government may be empowered to issue money, and allowed a monopoly in it. But the constitution may subject the grant of the monopoly to specifically-defined rules that limit the powers of the money-creation authority.

Two types of rules or directives command attention. First, a rule may specify directly-measurable quantities of nominal money. In the no-growth economy, the rule may specify that no money should be issued subsequent to an initial period. In a growing economy, the rule may state that the authority may expand the supply of money at a defined rate set at or near some projected rate of real growth in the economy. This type of rule is widely associated with Professor Milton Friedman, who has proposed it[1] both as an objective for discretionary government policy as well as a binding constitutional constraint. There may, of course, be several variants of a monetary growth rule, including one that specifies a range of rates for monetary growth rather than a single rate.

Monetary indexing for stability

A second rule may be defined in terms of ends rather than means. One such rule, advanced by Irving Fisher[2] and Henry Simons[3] among others, would direct the monetary authority to keep the value of the monetary unit stable, defined in terms of a designated index, which would require that the authority modify the quantity of money as necessary to accomplish this result. This rule, or some variant of it, has the advantage over

---

[1] For example, in' The Rôle of Monetary Policy', *American Economic Review*, March 1968, and *The Counter-Revolution in Monetary Theory*, Occasional Paper 33, IEA, 1970.

[2] Irving Fisher (assisted by Harry G. Brown), *The Purchasing Power of Money*, Macmillan, New York, 1912.

[3] Henry C. Simons, *Economic Policy for a Free Society*, University of Chicago Press, Chicago, 1948.

the Friedman-like rule of allowing for flexibility in adjusting the quantity of money to an unpredicted emergence of money substitutes such as credit cards, but it is relatively more difficult to monitor than the money-growth type of rule. The monetary authority could be judged only after the event, when perhaps the damage had been done, and it would prove difficult if not impossible to distinguish genuine error from deliberate subversion of the rule.

20. THE THREE STAGES OF MONETARY DEBATES

There are three separate stages of debate and analysis of monetary policy. These stages have not always been carefully distinguished one from the other, and controversies at one stage have tended to mask basic agreement at others. In distinguishing among the three stages, we will indicate precisely where our discussion belongs.

(1) *Discretionary monetary policy*
To the extent that political decision-makers have any latitude at all for discretion in their behaviour, the consequences of alternative courses of action may be analysed and discussed. The first stage of debates involves the week-by-week, month-by-month, year-by-year, or even government-by-government implementation of policy on monetary aggregates by the existing authority. The focus of the discussion is on what the legally-protected monetary monopolist 'should' do. What rate of expansion in the money supply should be followed? Should credit conditions be eased or tightened? Economists devote interminable effort to discussions of such questions without really understanding what rôle they are playing.

We do not suggest that the effort is wholly wasteful. Politicians and bureaucrats with decision-making power may pay some attention to the economists' arguments. But what must be recognised is that it is *persuasion* that is relevant, not the scientific validity or invalidity of this or that economic theory, not the moral superiority of this or that manner of behaving. Economists may impose some costs on the monetary monopolists by making them 'feel bad' by following their 'natural' tendencies towards generating real revenues through inflation, but these costs are likely to be dominated by the more direct incentives such as increased revenue. This predicted outcome will be emphasised by the recognition that not all economists will provide advice and counsel in the direction of lower rates of monetary expansion. Economists can always be found who will give evidence to support those directions of policy that coincide with the objectives of the real political revenue maximisers.

Our analysis and discussion in this *Paper* have little to do with this first stage of discourse.

(2) *The desirable monetary constitution*

A second stage of analysis, discussion, and debate, that should be sharply separated from the first, involves consideration of alternative constitutional-institutional régimes, more or less along the lines of the earlier treatment (pp. 59-63). Proponents of totally free markets in money argue with those who support the establishment of a commodity-based money, or a return to a gold reserve standard, and both groups argue with those who advance proposals for constitutionally-enforced money-growth or price-level stabilisation rules. Perhaps the most intense of such continuing arguments is that between the proponents of a gold-based commodity standard, the 'gold bugs', and the proponents of a fiat standard with constitutional safeguards.

The sharpness of the discord among the supporters and advocates of these two alternative régimes tends to overshadow and even to negate the basic agreement among all these groups at a third level of discourse, that concerning the desirability of a monetary constitution itself.

(3) *The desirability of a monetary constitution*

The proponents-advocates of free-market money, competitive monies, commodity money, or rule-constrained fiat issue *all* agree on the desirability, necessity, acceptability of *some monetary constitution*. Our argument in this *Hobart Paper* is exclusively devoted to this third stage. It is an argument for rules, in the familiar 'rules-versus-authority' debate. We have tried to be consistent in keeping clear of involvement in the other stages of the debates. We have not discussed alternative directions of monetary policy under discretionary authority of existing monetary monopolies.

[64]

We have offered no brief for one particular monetary constitution over others. Our charge is: Let us *first* agree that a monetary constitution is necessary *before* exhausting our energies in debates over the precise content of this constitution! Otherwise, the ship may sink while we debate which lifeboat to use.

Our brief is aimed to show that the absence of an explicit monetary constitution is unacceptable in any meaningful setting where the rules of social order are derived from the values held by citizens. To us it is indeed folly to confine analysis and discussion to examination of alternative lines of policy that are to be implemented by ordinary men and women who happen to find themselves in positions of political power. We should not, of course, deny that some such persons may be 'good men and true', but even victory in persuading one set of office holders to adopt 'our' preferred paths of monetary policy could only be short-lived.

Constitutional restraints, not 'advice', the only effective discipline on politicians

Experience should have taught us that direct economic advice to governments can be of relatively little lasting value. Men who make decisions in governmental rôles are ordinary mortals like the rest of us, and they will tend to be motivated by their own objectives instead of any 'truths' propounded by their economists. Once this simple point is recognised, our emphasis on *constitutional-institutional* change logically follows. Reforms in policy to be implemented by ordinary men can only come through reforms in the rules within which they operate.

We cannot, and should not, expect the decision-makers in the Bank of England or the United States Federal Reserve Board to behave 'as if' they are bound by a non-existent constitutional rule for money issue. They will behave in accordance with such a rule only if it exists. As the 1980s commence, more and more economists are coming to realise that unrestrained monetary monopoly is the *institutional* explanation of the great inflation of the 1970s. *Institutional* explanation suggests *institutional* reform. Only by restraining the discretionary powers of the monetary authorities through enforceable constitutional rules will the inflation be controlled. It is the *monetary régime,* not *monetary policy,* that must be modified.

[65]

QUESTIONS FOR DISCUSSION

1. What are the two 'market failure' arguments alleged to warrant not only a governmental rôle in defining and/or regulating the value of the monetary unit, but also a governmental monopoly over money creation?

2. 'Even slight attention to the relevance of normal political behaviour should have suggested that the Utopian Keynesian rule for fiscal policy would produce biases towards budget deficits.' Evaluate this proposition.

3. Do you find plausible the hypothesis that governments are 'malevolent despots' aiming to maximise the real revenues they can secure from their unrestricted monopoly in the issue of money?

4. 'The real value of the money issue to government will be the *transactions* value that money serves in the economy.' Explain.

5. How can a monopoly holder of the money-creation franchise extract more than the pure transactions value from citizens?

6. What factors limit the amount of real resources in excess of the pure transactions value which governments as monopoly revenue-maximisers will seek to extract?

7. Why will governments always secure more real revenue at *some* rate of inflation than under a simple non-inflationary régime?

8. 'Inflation is a *retroactive* and hence inescapable tax on money balances.' Discuss.

9. 'Only by restraining the discretionary powers of the monetary authorities through enforceable constitutional rules will inflation be controlled.' Do you agree?

10. What are the four schemes considered in the text which could constitute the substance of a monetary constitution? Evaluate their relative merits.

FURTHER READING

Bailey, Martin, 'The Welfare Cost of Inflation Finance', *Journal of Political Economy* 64 (April 1956), pp. 93-110.

> This is the classic paper on inflation as a tax. It deals with inflation in a setting where inflation rates are known *ex ante*, and is concerned to compare alternative inflationary régimes from a perspective of efficiency.

Brennan, Geoffrey, and Buchanan, James M., *The Power to Tax*, Cambridge University Press, 1980.

> This is a book-length treatment of the question of how the revenue powers of government might be constrained. Chapter VI deals with the money-creation power in a more analytical way than here, though along similar lines.

——, 'Revenue Implications of Inflation Under Leviathan', *Amer. Econ. Rev.*, May 1981, Papers & Proceedings (forthcoming).

> A brief discussion of the central elements of the argument outlined here, designed for the professional economist.

Buchanan, James M., Wagner, Richard E., and Burton, John, *The Economic Consequences of Mr Keynes*, Hobart Paper No. 78, Institute of Economic Affairs, London, 1978.

> This is an account for the non-economist of the political consequences of the pursuit of Keynesian policies that serves to lodge macro-economic stabilisation theory within a properly articulated theory of political process.

Cagan, Philip, 'The Monetary Dynamics of Hyper-Inflation', in Milton Friedman (ed.), *Studies In The Quantity Theory of Money*, University of Chicago Press, Chicago, 1956, pp. 25-110.

> This paper remains the classic for economists on hyper-inflationary experience.

Johnson, Harry G., 'A Note On the Dishonest Government and the Inflation Tax', *Journal of Monetary Economics*, 3 (July 1977), pp. 375-377.

> A short paper that tells a story of how the government might operate strategically to increase the revenues from inflation

under a particular set of assumptions about money-holders' expectations.

Niskanen, William, *Bureaucracy and Representative Government*, Aldine, Chicago, 1971.

This book sets out the now-standard economic theory of bureaucracy, from which in part the theory of politics used here derives.

Sjaastad, Larry, 'Why Stable Inflations Fail: An Essay in Political Economy', in Michael Parkin and George Zis (eds.), *Inflation And the World Economy*, Manchester University Press, Manchester, 1976.

A paper that is close in spirit to this one and the Johnson paper cited above, though more technical than either.